A Rug Hooker's Garden

**EDITION IV
OF RUG HOOKING
MAGAZINE'S
FRAMEWORK SERIES**

EDITOR
Patrice A. Crowley

BOOK DESIGNER
Cher Williams

PHOTOGRAPHY
Impact Xpozures
(except where indicated)

ASSISTANT EDITOR
Brenda J. Wilt

PUBLISHER
M. David Detweiler

PRESENTED BY

R·U·G HOOKING

1300 Market Street, Suite 202
Lemoyne, PA 17043-1420
(717) 234-5091
(800) 233-9055
www.rughookingonline.com

TABLE OF CONTENTS

The Flowers

ADDITIONAL INSTRUCTION AND DESIGN HINTS

EDITOR'S NOTE

"How do I hook a flower?" That is the question most commonly asked of the staff of *Rug Hooking*, and the reason for this edition of our Framework Series.

Whether it's a lily, a rose, or a pansy, a hooked flower poses its own trials and triumphs. *A Rug Hooker's Garden* is like having a master gardener tending your real flower beds—the authors of this book have made hooked flowers their passion, and their wisdom and experience is here to help you from bud to blossom.

It's one thing to read instructions on how to hook a flower and another to see the resulting element in full color. Thanks to the beautiful examples presented with each chapter of this book, you can see how each flower blooms, so to speak, from the first loop to the last. The chapters on designing and dyeing provide further help for those eager to sow their own hooked garden. And the basic hooking lessons and glossary can assist the neophyte.

Every gardener worth her green thumb has more than one kind of garden. As a rug hooker, you can expand upon your formal flowers to include more rustic, primitive ones or even imaginary ones by reading the chapters on those topics.

Gardens are meant to be gorgeous, and hooked ones never sprout weeds. May *A Rug Hooker's Garden* germinate the seeds of inspiration in your mind and get you to grow your next flowers with wool.

—*Patrice Crowley*

ABOUT THE PUBLISHER

Rug Hooking magazine, the publisher of *A Rug Hooker's Garden*, welcomes you to the rug hooking community. Since 1989 *Rug Hooking* has served thousands of rug hookers around the world with its instructional, illustrated articles on dyeing, designing, color planning, hooking techniques, and more. Each issue of the magazine contains color photographs of beautiful rugs old and new, profiles of teachers, designers, and fellow rug hookers, and announcements of workshops, exhibits, and gatherings.

Rug Hooking has responded to its readers' demand for more inspiration and information by establishing an inviting, informative website at www.rughookingonline.com and by publishing a number of books on this fiber art. Along with how-to pattern books and a *Sourcebook* listing of teachers, guilds, and schools, *Rug Hooking* has produced the competition-based book series *A Celebration of Hand-Hooked Rugs*, now in its tenth year. *A Rug Hooker's Garden* is part of *Rug Hooking*'s popular Framework Series of in-depth educational books.

The hand-hooked rugs you'll see in *A Rug Hooker's Garden* represent just a fragment of the incredible art that is being produced today by women and men of all ages. For more information on rug hooking and *Rug Hooking* magazine, call or write us at the address on page 1.

MEET THE AUTHORS
BY BRENDA WILT

MARLETA ANDERSON

Marleta Anderson, of Newark Valley, New York, has been hooking rugs for more than 15 years. She enjoys working in both fine and wide cuts, and especially likes to use recycled wool in her rugs. Her work has been exhibited at the Tioga County Fair and at several McGown* guild shows. Marleta demonstrates hooking at the Newark Valley Historical Society Museum.

BJ ANDREAS

BJ Andreas is no shrinking violet when it comes to hooking flowers. Living in Florida's bright sunshine has taught her to hook in bold hues to minimize the effects of fading. BJ has been hooking for more than two decades and teaches at various camps. She is the director of two workshops in the southeastern United States.

MARTHA BEALS

Having grown up in a family of needleworkers, Martha Beals took naturally to rug hooking. She's been hooking since 1994 when she sought an art form that allowed her to be creative. Martha is a certified McGown instructor who has overcome a fear of dyeing to create her own palette for her hooked art. She holds classes in her home in Sidney, Maine.

NANCY BLOOD

A rug hooker for the past 20 years, Nancy Blood, of Owego, New York, teaches hooking in her home and at various camps and workshops around the United States. Known for her expertise in dyeing and color planning, she works with interior designers to customize rooms and rugs. Nancy is a certified McGown teacher and the editor of the national McGown guild's newsletter. She is also a frequent contributor to *Rug Hooking* and a member of its editorial board.

CONNIE CHARLESON

Over the last four decades, Connie Charleson has developed a specialty in hooking finely shaded flowers. The Stratton-certified** instructor teaches at rug camps and opens her home in New Port Richey, Florida, for periodic workshops and individual instruction. Connie is the author of the self-published dye book *Connie's Cauldron*.

HELEN CONNELLY

Helen Connelly, of Northport, New York, has been hooking for about 35 years and teaching for 30. She is a McGown-certified instructor who teaches in her home and at camps and workshops. Helen is a past president of the McGown guild and of the Northern Teachers Workshop. She counts flowers and pictorials among her favorite subjects to hook. **SANDY BROWN**, of Pittsburgh, Pennsylvania, herself a McGown-certified instructor, interviewed Helen and observed her at work to write some of the articles in this book.

JEANNE FALLIER

A founding member of ATHA***, Jeanne Fallier, of Westford, Massachusetts, has been hooking, designing, and teaching for more than four decades. Jeanne has her own design business, The Rugging Room. She has written for *Rug Hooking* and is a member of the publication's editorial board.

JANE MCGOWN FLYNN

The granddaughter of Pearl K. McGown, Jane McGown Flynn is the chairman of the board of the national McGown guild. Before her retirement in 1999, Jane ran a mail-order pattern business and organized the McGown teachers workshops. Her patterns, now distributed by Charco Inc., remain popular among rug hookers both novice and expert. Jane continues to hook from her New Hampshire home.

SUSAN HIGGINS

Susan Higgins, of San Francisco, California, chairs the kinesiology department at San Francisco State University and has been hooking since the early 1990s. Susan is partial to dramatic colors and bold designs and enjoys a variety of styles and techniques. Her work has appeared in *Rug Hooking* magazine and in editions of *A Celebration of Hand-Hooked Rugs*.

BETTY MCCLENTIC

A certified McGown teacher, Betty McClentic, of Warwick, Rhode Island, has been hooking rugs for 30 years. Betty teaches in her home and at rug schools and offers regular classes in students' homes. She has been director of the McGown Northern Teachers Workshop since 1989.

*National Guild of Pearl K. McGown Rug
  Hookrafters, Inc.*
** *Charlotte Kimball Stratton's school*
*** *Association of Traditional Hooking Artists*

Betty McClentic

Helen Connelly

Jeanne Fallier

Martha Beals

Susan Higgins

Jane Flynn

Connie Charleson

Nancy Blood

BJ Andreas

Sandra L. Brown

THE FLOWERS

Chrysanthemum

HOOKING A CHRYSANTHEMUM, with all its petals, is a challenge. Because its petals overlap and curve you must complete each one before going on to the next.

The chrysanthemum I chose to hook is called *Indian Summer*. For it I used 10 values—8 values of a transitional swatch in an old rose hue and 2 values of a yellow for the bright tips (my dye formulas are below). It is not imperative that you use a transitional swatch, but it is necessary to have a good range of values from light to dark.

When I teach, I use a color-plan sketch that primarily uses colors rather than numbers to indicate the placement of values (see the illustration). Each color represents a *value* of a swatch—not the hue you are to use. It is much easier to follow a line of color than it is to look for a multitude of little numbers.

Begin hooking with the inside of the petal in the lower right corner, above the leaf and near the words (see the illustration). Start with the darkest value (8) and hook directionally, moving outward with values 7, 6, and 5. For the outer curve use values 1 and 2 of the yellow (shown as numbers in the illustration) blended into values 1, 2, 3, and 4 of the transitional swatch.

INDIAN SUMMER, 11" x 14", #2- AND 3-CUT WOOL ON WOOL. DESIGNED AND HOOKED BY CONNIE CHARLESON, NEW PORT RICHEY, FLORIDA. UNFINISHED.

Be sure to make an overlapping tip or edge lighter than what is beneath it in order to delineate the front and back of the petal or the inside and outside. The little sections marked with an X are at least two values darker than value 8; for them I used a few strands of leftover wool. If you can't find anything appropriate, then dye 1 strip 2 values darker than an 8.

With a transitional swatch I found it difficult to separate the center grouping of petals so they would not appear too rusty in color. So I ran value 5 through the cutter once with a #2 blade. This thin line sufficiently separated the petals, which were hooked with a #3 cut of wool. I did the same with the yellows and used those narrow strips for highlighting and separating petals.

For realistic shading you should also finger the values so they mesh. Fingering allows a smoother transition from one value to the next.

When hooking a single flower I often use wool for the backing, as I did here. Choose a color that complements the color of the flower you are hooking. For this chrysanthemum I used Dorr's celery wool. There's no need to hook the background when it is wool. It can be used as is or dip dyed before the pattern is printed on it.

I always use the open pan method of dyeing. I simmer my wool for 45 minutes after it comes to a boil.

CONNIE CHARLESON

FORMULA #19

This formula is for the yellow swatch. You will need 2 pieces of 6" x 12" white wool, 1 measuring cup, measuring spoons, and 3 Cushing brand dyes, Lemon, Canary, and Old Gold. The formula is for use in open pan dyeing.

Mix together $1/4$ teaspoon of Lemon, $1/8$ teaspoon of Canary, and $1/64$ teaspoon of Old Gold in $3/4$ cup of water. For value 1 use 1 $1/4$ teaspoons of dye; for value 2 use 2 $1/2$ teaspoons. Use 1 $1/2$ quarts of water per value.

FORMULA #203

This formula is for the transitional swatch. You will need 8 pieces of 6" x 12" white wool, 2 measuring cups, measuring spoons, and 2 Cushing dyes, Aqualon Yellow and Old Rose. The formula is for open pan dyeing.

In the first measuring cup add $1/16$ teaspoon of Aqualon Yellow to 1 cup plus 2 Tablespoons of water. In the second measuring cup add $1/8$ teaspoon of Old Rose to 1 cup plus 2 Tablespoons of water. Use 1$1/2$ quarts of water per value.

VALUE	YELLOW	OLD ROSE
1	2 Tbsp + 1 tsp	$1/4$ tsp
2	2 Tbsp + 1 tsp	$1/2$ tsp
3	2 Tbsp + 1 tsp	1 tsp
4	2 Tbsp + 1 tsp	2 tsp
5	2 Tbsp + 1 tsp	1 Tbsp + 1 tsp
6	2 Tbsp + 1 tsp	2 Tbsp + 1 tsp
7	2 Tbsp + 1 tsp	4 Tbsp + 1 tsp
8	1 Tbsp + 1 tsp	8 Tbsp + 1 tsp

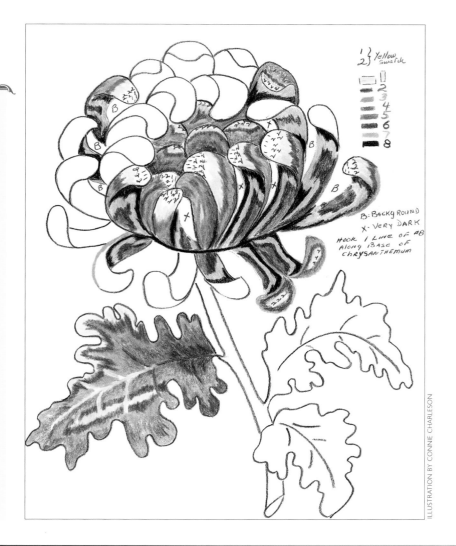

THE FLOWERS

POTPOURRI, 36" x 25", #3-CUT WOOL ON BURLAP. DESIGNED BY EDANA (QUAIL HILL DESIGNS). HOOKED BY MARLETA ANDERSON, NEWARK VALLEY, NEW YORK, 1984.

DAFFODILS AND NARCISSUS are considered cup-and-saucer flowers because their cupped center blossom is surrounded by a saucer of petals. My example of a yellow daffodil (which can range from pale cream to bright orange) is from the rug *Potpourri*. My teacher for the project was Arlene Cull and the dyeing was done by Nancy Blood. The dye formula used is Barbara Sleeper's #3H and runs from a light to a dark gold in eight values (value 1 being the lightest).

No matter what flower you are doing, think of it as painting with wool. Look at paintings and drawings of flowers and observe the areas of light and shadow. Exaggerating its shadows gives shape to a daffodil. To get a better idea of how your flower should be hooked, trace it on paper and shade it with a black pencil.

The most difficult part of hooking a daffodil or any other yellow flower is that yellow is hard to work with. It does not shade itself as easily as other colors. As my teacher always says, yellow is the color of sunshine, and you can't shade that. Therefore, the yellow you choose must have a deep eighth value and no jumps between values.

In hooking any flower, start with the petal that is in front of the others; in this case, the frill

"Fair Daffodils we weep to see You haste away so soon."

Robert Herrick

around the top of the daffodil's cup is predominant. Use the lightest value in the center of the frill, using only one or two darker values to fill the section. Hook in a few dark streaks from the edge toward the center to give a ruffled look to the frill. Use your darkest value to give depth to the inside of the cup. (I also placed a couple loops of green in the center to mimic stamens.) Fill in the rest of the frill with the other values.

Place value 8 under the frill on the outside of the cup to indicate the shadow cast by the frill. Notice that the shadow extends onto the petals on either side of it. The rest of my cup has a bit of value 1 near the center for a highlight, with the other values filling around it to the edges of the cup.

Hook the saucer with dark values at the base of each petal and where a shadow would be cast by one petal overlapping its neighbor. Also put some of the darker values in the center of the petals, but only enough to make it look like a fold is there, not a vein. The farther back the petals are the darker they should be to give shape and perspective to the flower.

If your flower rests on a light background, keep the lighter values toward the center of the petals with touches of the darker toward the edges, so the petals will not be lost against the background. The center of the throat should still be dark, however.

Marleta Anderson

THE FLOWERS

Daisy

FLORAL MEDLEY, 54" X 38", #3-CUT WOOL ON MONK'S CLOTH. DESIGNED AND HOOKED BY CONNIE CHARLESON, NEW PORT RICHEY, FLORIDA. UNFINISHED.

THE DAISY, LIKE THE PURPLE coneflower (*Echinacea purpurea*), black-eyed Susan, and some chrysanthemum varieties, is a flower with a central disk surrounded by many petals. The common white daisy (*Chrysanthemum leucanthemum*) and the painted daisy (pyrethrum) have flat, yellow centers. Black-eyed Susans have deep brown centers, and echinacea have deep rose-red ones. The swan-river daisy (*Brachycome iberidifolia*), an Australian annual, has a center of yellow and deep brown rimmed with blue petals. As you can tell, both as hookers and gardeners we have a variety of colors to choose from for our gardens.

The daisy, black-eyed Susan, coneflower, and all other single-petaled flowers are similarly hooked. Changing the color and shape of the center is all that is needed to change one flower to another. The daisy and single dahlias both have flat centers, while echinacea and black-eyed Susans have cone-shaped ones.

To hook a white daisy's center, use a yellow checked material around its base and a golden-yellow for the rest of it. Use a dark brown check and a dark, bronze-brown wool for the cone-shaped center of a black-eyed Susan.

To understand how to hook a daisy you must understand how to correctly portray the ways one petal can overlap another. That is, you must be able to discern which petal is on top or which edge is over another. My illustration will help you with four possible petal placements and their shading. For each of the four possibilities there are a number of examples shown. (This illustration uses colors rather than numbers to indicate the placement of values. Each color represents a *value* of a swatch—not the hue you are to use.)

When you have a top petal with both edges over another petal, make both of its edges light (see the petals marked #1). If the left side of the petal rests atop another and the right side is tucked underneath, shade as seen in petals designated #2. If the right side of the petal is on top and the left side is tucked underneath, shade as in the petals numbered #3. When a petal is tucked under at both edges, hook it like the petals marked #4.

WHITE TO GREEN

In 1 1/2 cups of boiling water mix together the following dyes:
1/4 tsp Lemon
1/64 tsp Bright Green
1/64 tsp Silver Gray
Use the chart below to add the proper amount of dye solution to 1 1/2 quarts of water per value. Let the water come to a boil, then let it simmer for 45 minutes.

VALUE	DYE	VALUE	DYE
1	1 tsp	4	2 Tbsp + 1 tsp
2	2 tsp		
3	2 Tbsp + 1 tsp	5	4 Tbsp + 1 tsp
		6	7 Tbsp

If you wish the first shade to be lighter, prepare 7 pieces of fabric and use the same formula in 1 1/2 cups of boiling water, but use this chart:

VALUE	DYE	VALUE	DYE
1	1/2 tsp	5	2 Tbsp + 1 tsp
2	1 tsp	6	4 Tbsp + 1 tsp
3	2 tsp		
4	1 Tbsp + 1 tsp	7	7 Tbsp

WHITE TO BLUE

Dissolve 1/16 teaspoon of Black in 1 1/2 cups of boiling water. Then use the following chart to apportion the dye solution:

VALUE	DYE	VALUE	DYE
1	1/8 tsp	4	1 tsp
2	1/4 tsp	5	2 tsp
3	1/2 tsp	6	4 tsp

WHITE TO GRAY

Dissolve 1/16 teaspoon of Silver Gray in 1 1/2 cups of boiling water. Use the white-to-blue chart to apportion the dyes.

Here are open-pan dyeing formulas for daisies shaded from white to green, white to blue, or white to gray. For all three formulas you will need 6 pieces of 6" x 12" white wool, 2 measuring cups, measuring spoons, and Cushing dyes.

CONNIE CHARLESON

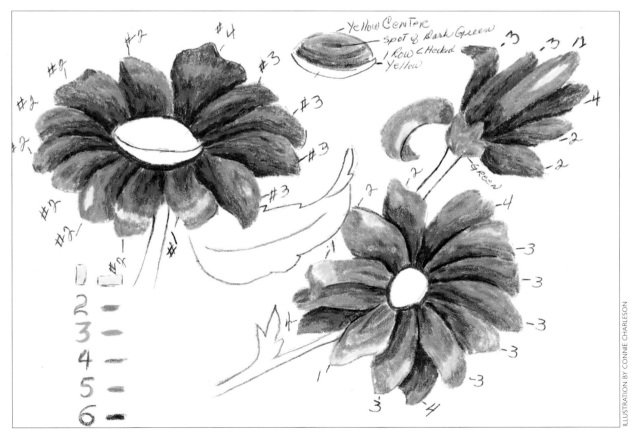

THE FLOWERS

Geranium

AFRICA'S GIFT, **43" x 28"**, #3-CUT WOOL ON 2 X 2 COTTON. DESIGNED BY JANE MCGOWN FLYNN. HOOKED BY NANCY BLOOD, OWEGO, NEW YORK, 1997.

GERANIUMS, WITH THEIR individual florets and variegated foliage, present to the rug hooker both a test of her skills and an opportunity to create an unusual floral design. The colors and characteristics of geraniums are so varied that a rug hooker should have no difficulty finding the perfect plant for a scene or still life. Some are trailing, others are short; some sport vivid flowers, while others bear unusual foliage that is more striking than the flowers.

When hooking the individual florets of geraniums, be sure to use great contrast—deep darks and light lights. Don't mess with middle values. However, in my *Africa's Gift* rug, I used more medium tones than I usually do. I started the top petals with light values and moved to the dark, and then began the underneath petals with the dark and ended with the middle values. I skipped no values and always began with value 1 or 8.

Because my red swatch was so intense, I thought I'd have to add a deeper burgundy to the shadows, but it wasn't necessary. I did some subtle shading in the florets and beneath the flower globes by placing strokes of color in different areas and in varying amounts.

I try to use my swatches efficiently by moving through all eight values; I never depend on just the middle ones. The leaves are combinations of mock shading and

> ## "I HAVE LOVED FLOWERS THAT FADE,
> ## WITHIN WHOSE MAGIC TENTS
> ## RICH HUES HAVE MARRIAGE MADE
> ## WITH SWEET UNMEMORIED SCENTS."
>
> ROBERT BRIDGES

stroking (fingering). I laid in the bones (around the veins) with rows of successive values and then fingered my way to the edges.

For the leaves I deliberately chose two closely related green swatch formulas and used the same wool to dye both. One swatch tends toward the emerald, while the other is more olive. I could have chosen one swatch formula and dyed over a larger variety of wools, but that would have made basically the same color, and I wanted more diversity.

The turned-over parts of the leaves were shaded in leaf colors, given their size and importance. Always extend the outer edges of a turnover so the motif doesn't look like it's wearing a hat. This elongates the leaf's graceful lines and connects the two parts of the element.

The horseshoe marking on the leaves I hooked randomly with no attempt at being symmetrical. I used a brown spot with rosy tones, which reflects the red of the flowers; the complementary green around it helps keep it brown. Veins were dyed over yellow wool and have flashes of rosiness—subtle, yet apparent.

NANCY BLOOD

THE FLOWERS

Hibiscus

CARIB, 54" X 29", #3-CUT WOOL ON 2 X 2 COTTON. DESIGNED BY JANE MCGOWN FLYNN. HOOKED BY MARTHA BEALS, SIDNEY, MAINE, 1998.

HIBISCUS, FROM THE GREEK *hibiskos*, a mallow, has many names, such as rose of China and shoe-black plant. Hibiscus flowers are delicate and translucent and bear ruffles, valleys, and rises that need a rug hooker's careful attention. Look for good examples of the flower you are hooking in books, nature, or paintings (watercolors are especially helpful with shading).

Hibiscus blossoms come in many color combinations, and dyeing for them is the most exciting part of creating them in wool. You can dye single- or multiple-color swatches from 6 to 10 values. Or you could dip dye your wool, making such dazzling combi-

nations as a red at one end of the strip to a yellow at the other. Cross-swatching works well, also—when you change from one color to another, make the change

where the value of both colors is the same.

Always hook the object in the foreground first. Here, that means the petal that rests on top of all

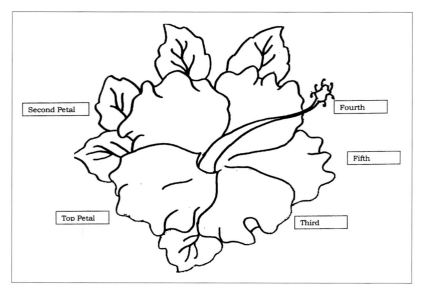

"EVERY FLOWER OF THE FIELD...CAN—IF DULY CONSIDERED—READ US LECTURES OF ETHICS OR DIVINITY."

SIR THOMAS POPE BLOUNT

the others (see the illustration). This top petal should be the brightest and boldest. Start in the center of the flower with your next-to-darkest value and work outward, fingering this value in with progressively lighter ones. Hook in the direction that the flower petal grows.

As you approach the petal's ruffled edge, plan ahead so dark values can fall in between the ruffles. Shade the ruffles in a V shape (you can draw the V on your pattern), placing your dark value in the middle of the V and working outward to the light shades at the edge of the ruffle.

Don't be afraid to use your lightest and darkest values for highlights and shadows, for they give your flower depth and brilliance. Veins commonly show through on hibiscus petals, so hook them in to lend realism.

If the stamen rests on the top petal, hook it before you hook the petal. The stamen is usually the same color as the flower. Hook it in light values with a highlight for its contours. Don't let it over-

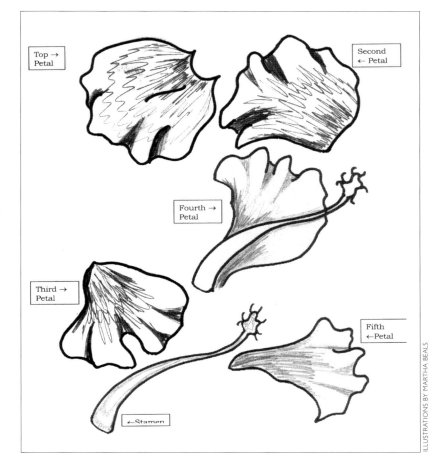

whelm the petals. The anther (at its tip) is a translucent yellow.

As you hook the second petal, place your dark value along the edge that touches the top petal. This dark edge makes the petal look as if it rests beneath the top petal. Hook the opposite edge in a lighter value to give it height and distinguish it from the next petal

down. Each succeeding petal is done the same way except for your last petal, which usually is the darkest and beneath all the other petals. Use your darkest values for the majority of this petal, lightening a little on the edge.

MARTHA BEALS

THE FLOWERS

Hydrangea

RAPTURE, 72" x 44", #3- AND 4-CUT WOOL ON 2 x 2 COTTON. DESIGNED BY JANE McGOWN FLYNN. HOOKED BY HELEN CONNELLY, NORTHPORT, NEW YORK. UNFINISHED.

HYDRANGEA, LIKE HYACINTHS, lupines, and lilacs, are considered clustered flowers, which bear a mass of small blossoms. The difficulty in hooking clustered flowers is knowing how to make a distinct separation between the flowerets. The key is the artful use of color. For example, even though you may think of lilacs as a cluster of light- to dark-purple flowers, try to inject other hues into that gradation by using a swatch of reddish purple to light blue or perhaps periwinkle-blue to light purple, thereby giving yourself several options for hooking each cluster.

By choosing colors on either side of purple on the color wheel (such as a blue-purple and a red-purple) and using two to three swatches in each cluster, you can create the overall sense of a purple flower, as the eye will blend the colors in viewing it. Having a couple of light, medium, and dark swatches to choose from as the cluster is being hooked separates the flowerets better than if you use only one swatch. Borrowing light and dark values from closely hued swatches is called multiswatching; it is one of the tricks of advanced hooking and provides more visual interest to a rug than does the use of a single-hued swatch.

To begin hooking a clustered flower, determine which general direction the lights to darks are

going. (Do they run from the top of the cluster to the bottom? Front spine to back sides? Both?) Start hooking the lightest-value flowerets. Since these flowerets are usually so small, there won't be much opportunity for shading in each petal. Some clustered flowers have a center that can be hooked with a loop or two of bright chartreuse-yellow (put this in before you start the petals). Make certain that not every floweret gets a center. Once the lightest-value flowerets are done, hook the medium-value ones, again choosing from whatever swatch allows you to hook two side-by-side flowerets without losing

contrast. Finally, hook the darkest flowerets, preferably with unusual colors—even bright or poison

ones—that can be found elsewhere in the rug.

The background for these small flowers will either be the rest of the cluster or the background of the rug (which will make some of the flowerets appear to float from the cluster). Hook the gaps between the petals with a medium-value wool, preferably a softly spot-dyed one (purples are best for shadows, but any wool carried over from elsewhere in the rug, even from a leaf, would be good). Hook in darker wool at the darker end of the cluster. A single row of hooking around the flowerets is usually sufficient.

HELEN CONNELLY
(WITH SANDRA BROWN)

THE FLOWERS

Iris

WHEN YOU THINK OF AN IRIS, think of the number three: There are three outspread petals known as falls, three upright petals called standards, and three stamens. The falls are usually spotted, veined, or marked in some other way and sport a beard—a textured cleft.

Dip dye or casserole dye your wool for the more colorful and highly streaked iris varieties. Or overdye colored wool in blue, yellow, pink, or light green. The falls are often hooked in darker or different colors than the standards, but to unify the hues place the wool for the falls in the same dye bath as you are using for the standards.

Hook the beard first, usually with a bright yellow or orange wool. Then turn your attention to the frilly parts of the petals.

One of the keys to hooking an iris is carefully rendering the ruffles and the turned-over portions of the blossoms (called turnovers). Hook the turnovers first on the forwardmost petal, usually with the lightest values,

so the shadow the petal casts can be hooked into the petals behind it. After hooking the turnover, put in a darker shadow line (never in a single value or a straight line) beneath the first petal on the petal below it.

To faithfully depict a ruffle, with its uneven, papery quality, shade the hills and valleys of the petal edges. Hook with lighter values on the top of each ruffle and proceed downward with darker ones. These darker valleys can also be carried to the base of the petal, conveying the striation one sees in irises.

Then hook the rest of the petal, with a line down the center to set the general direction of your loops. This center line can be a different value or color than the rest of the petal and should be more of a triangle widening at the bottom than a single line. It can either be shaded into the rest of the petal or not, depending on how much contrast is desired. Depending on whether you use dip-dyed or swatch-gradation wool, this shaded area will usually be blended (fingered) into lighter areas on the main part of the petal

SWEET SIXTEEN, 12" x 42 1/2", #3-CUT WOOL ON 2 x 2 COTTON. DESIGNED BY JANE MCGOWN FLYNN. HOOKED BY HELEN CONNELLY, NORTHPORT, NEW YORK, 1994.

before going back to shadow at the base. It's important to provide contrast between the petals and the center of the iris, so don't be afraid to jump four to five values between the edges of the petals and the inside of the blossom.

Highlights are hooked as bright spots where the petal would pick up the light (these highlights are never perfect circles or squares, just randomly shaped). Always hook them with your lightest value. Finger the value to the darker areas by reverting to soft pastels such as celery, pink, or yellow. Finish up with a row of background around the entire flower that's hooked close to the petals to sharpen them.

HELEN CONNELLY
(WITH SANDRA BROWN)

IMPERFECT BEAUTY

Nothing in nature is symmetrical or perfect. Therefore, never make motifs in a design identical to each other— no two roses, no two peaches, no two leaves, and so on. In fact, no hooked piece should look like any other hooked piece. That's the beauty of what we do—there are infinite variations we can achieve. Strive for those variations.—*Nancy Blood*

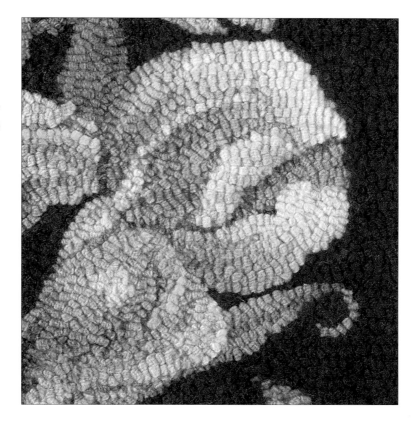

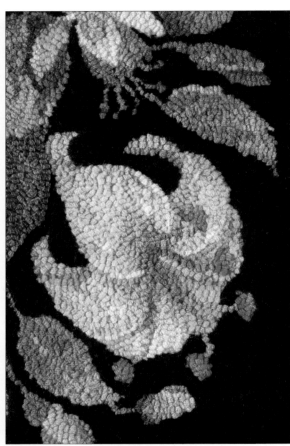

SWEET SIXTEEN, DETAIL. DESIGNED BY JANE MCGOWN FLYNN. HOOKED BY HELEN CONNELLY. SEE THE FULL BELLPULL ON PAGES 16 AND 19.

LILIES ARE CONSIDERED ONE of the throated flowers because of their trumpet shape. Before hooking one of them decide whether the throat (center) of the flower is going to be light or dark; that helps determine the treatment for the petals. Typically the petals are hooked in a different value than the throat, so that if the throat is light the petals are medium or dark.

Hooking a lily gives you an excellent opportunity to use dip-dyed or casserole-dyed wool. With them you can dye the wool the colors of the petal from light to dark and then simply hook from one end of the petal to another.

Put the pistils, stamens, and anthers in first. Hook them either in bright chartreuse or another bright color that needs to be carried around

the rug. This is a good place for poison—those extremely bright colors of wool that make the entire piece exciting.

The petals are hooked in the order in which they appear to the viewer—the forwardmost petal first, secondmost petals second, and so on. This allows shadow areas created by the petals on top to be hooked onto the petals below, thereby creating depth.

Additionally, make the forwardmost petals lighter in value than those in the rear. In your dye pot include light wools for the top petals, and increasingly darker wools for the rear ones. For example, use white, natural, or pale pink for the front petals, then salmon or yellow for middle ones, and blues, orange-tans, or dull golds for rear ones.

If you are using swatches, start with the petals' highlights in the lightest value of any swatch used elsewhere in the rug. To help you place a highlight properly, draw an irregular shape on the petal, usually in two places on either side of a central vein. That shape becomes the highlight that all other values are fingered (blended) into, extending into either a dark or light throat. Begin hooking the rest of the petal in the center after the smile line is set (this is the line which delineates the curve of the front petal—we look past this line to see into the throat). If the throat is dark, hook this smile line in lighter values; if the throat is light, hook it in darker values. Hook the remainder of the petal from the center out.

Borrow colors from adjacent flowers to hook any turned-over parts of the lily's petals. Remember that, with the amount of hybridizing out there, a lily can be almost any color.

HELEN CONNELLY
(WITH SANDRA BROWN)

"I KNOW A LITTLE GARDEN CLOSE,

SET THICK WITH LILY AND RED ROSE,

WHERE I WOULD WANDER IF I MIGHT

FROM DEWY MORN TO DEWY NIGHT."

WILLIAM MORRIS

THE FLOWERS

Morning Glory

MORNING GLORIES, 11" x 13 1/2", #3-CUT WOOL ON MONK'S CLOTH. DESIGNED BY JANE McGOWN FLYNN. HOOKED BY NANCY BLOOD, OWEGO, NEW YORK, 2000.

MORNING GLORIES ARE ONE OF my favorite flowers to hook. I think of them as little bits of fallen sky, so I like them crisp with blueness.

Because they are throated flowers (those that have a throat, or tube, at their center), morning glories can often pose some of the most difficult hooking problems. You must be able to give the throat the appearance of depth and also have the petal rest atop the throat. One way to achieve this look is to think of the part of the petal closest to you as a lip—one that's pouting. Use the three lightest values of an 8-value swatch to make the lip pout by stroking short, curved lines along the length of this lip. Start with

"THE MORNING GLORY OPENS BLUE AND COOL ON A HOT MORNING."

DENISE LEVERTOV

value 1, then 2, then 3. If needed, value 4 can also be used, but go no deeper than value 5—save the darker values for the throat.

After most of the lip is done, work your way from the throat to the edges of the petal. I use fingers of the darkest values to fill in the throat, working in a fan shape. The medium values in the throat will match those used on the front lip, tying the two halves together. As you continue to the edge of the flower, use the lighter values. By stroking in the values, you can pleat and fold the petals at will.

Note that the lower left morning glory in my interpretation of *Morning Glories* is lighter and more conservative than the other ones, yet you can still get into its depths. The upper left petal is more dramatic—it was about this time I saw I was beginning to run out of the lighter values of my swatch. Because I still had another flower and all the buds to do, I played more with the shading. The last blossom, on the right, is rather flamboyant (I played a lot); it is the most striking of the three flowers, I believe. Notice that the values in it do not touch one another in numerical sequence.

Morning glory buds, believe it or not, are hooked like ropes. Because they are so twisty, I always extend their sides (like turned-over leaves) so that each little segment is attached to its neighbor. Buds are often a soft pink-white, even in blue morning

glories, and it would not be wrong to do the throat in this color, since that part is what shows of the bud after the flower has opened.

NANCY BLOOD

THE FLOWERS

Orchid

ORCHIDS, 23" x 17", #3-CUT WOOL ON COTTON. ADAPTED FROM A PAINTING BY ALEXANDRE BRUN AND HOOKED BY SUSAN HIGGINS, SAN FRANCISCO, CALIFORNIA, 1999.

ORCHIDS ARE BOTH ELEGANT and mysterious, coming from the darkest reaches of Africa, Asia, and South America. Orchids evoke images of exotic, haunting beauty and perfection. When I hook an orchid, I try to capture the seductiveness of this flower amid its dark and luxurious setting, yet be true to the structure of the flower. To me, this is the art of hooking.

All orchids have three elongated sepals and three fuller petals, one of which is distinct. This distinct petal (called the lip) varies in size, color, or shape from the other petals. A good visual aid of the flower allows you to study the color of the specimen and its characteristics. Look at paintings, flower catalogs, and field guides. Better yet, photograph a flower or purchase one in full bloom and use it as a reference.

I based my *Orchids* piece on a watercolor and began working on it in collaboration with Helen Connelly. The dendrobium orchid depicted in it is white with pink tips. The white-frilled lip has both a magenta throat and interior. The sepals are elongated and rather straight, while the petals are large and curvaceous.

Closely examine your visual aid's colors and range of intensities. Then search through your wool and select the colors that match this array. Orchids are a good flower for using leftover wool from other projects. The flowers are fairly small and don't take much wool to hook. In *Orchids* my palette consisted of various shades of pale chartreuse, taupe, gray-violet, dirty mauve, hot pink, muted pink, brown-pink, burgundy, salmon, and magenta. For the whites I included a swatch of pure white to lavender-gray white, a swatch of pure white to beige-white, and odds and ends of browned, pinked, and greened whites.

Start hooking with the foremost petal (the one nearest to you, the viewer). Decide on the direction of the light source to plan the shadows and highlights. Examine your visual aid to see how the petals cast a shadow on those beneath or behind them. The lightest values fall on the highest point of an object. As the object recedes, these progress to medium values and ultimately to dark ones in grooves and the base.

Hook your brightest white for this petal's highlights (use the brightest value in your wool—this will be the base line from which you judge all other intensities). Hook highlights in clear, distinct, well-shaped paths that follow the contour of the flower. Then hook the next brightest color and so on until you are hooking the darkest. The shape of the petal and the size and extent of the high points determine where

the shadows fall, either within one petal or between petals. Hook the shadows after the highlights are placed. Now hook the next-closest petal in the same way. Look at the two petals and see if the intensities you selected achieved good contrast between them.

When hooking the lip, follow the same process as for the other petals. Lay down clean, clear high-

lights along the contour. Shade the highlights. The last thing you will hook is the dark, magenta center and throat. Note that the magenta is deepest at its base and progresses to a paler pink that is a bit jagged in appearance, and that the white that protrudes into the center is often dulled. Notice that the lip, petal, and tips all have variations in color.

SUSAN HIGGINS

THE FLOWERS

Padula

FASCINATION, 12' X 9', #8-CUT WOOL ON BURLAP. DESIGNED BY
LIB CALLAWAY. HOOKED BY BJ ANDREAS, MIAMI, FLORIDA, 1994.

PEARL K. McGOWN INVENTED the term *padula* to describe a make-believe flower. A padula only exists in the minds of the designer and hooker, and it is transformed into anything either person would like it to be. I can only imagine why Pearl added these imaginary flowers to her elegant, formal, realistic patterns. Perhaps she included them to have a bit of whimsy interspersed among her intricate flowers. Padulas help me balance colors when I want to add more of a favorite value in a rug or add a brighter, more intense value of an already present color.

A padula can be a barely recognizable version of a real flower, such as a throated flower. Or it can be as shapeless as a lady's housecoat blowing in the breeze. Perhaps padulas have finally come into their own with the renewed popularity of primitive designs. In *Fascination*, a primitive rug, almost every flower could be called a padula except for the center's two roses. Among the flowers are throated padulas—certainly not morning glories or hibiscus, but throated flowers nonetheless.

I enjoy hooking padulas because with them I'm not tied down to using realistic colors, which fits in with the primitive rugs I hook. The center field of *Fascination* holds about 80 padulas. The first border next to this area has 18 clusters of three padulas totaling 54. For those two areas I had the entire color wheel to select from. But color planning the outside border had me stumped. Its 71 padulas were the biggest challenge of the entire rug. I decided I would simply follow the color wheel all the way around the border and that would add some symmetry to it.

The center of an individual padula can make or break the flower. Some hookers like them sedate and quiet, but I like mine to make a statement, adding pizzazz and often a few loops of poison to a rug. I don't want a bull's eye, but a center that will draw the eye to the flower. Centers are a perfect place for checks, tweeds, and plaids. I also use textures (different ones) to outline the padula. Textures make a padula, with its simple design, interesting.

Adding that interest through selecting the right wool is what makes padulas so much fun to hook. It doesn't matter what they look like as long as you like them. And perhaps that was what Pearl had intended. She wanted us to use our imagination and make padulas whatever we wanted them to be.

BJ ANDREAS

THE FLOWERS
Pansy

PANSY AND SLATE WALLHANGING, 11" x 11", #3-CUT WOOL ON MONK'S CLOTH. DESIGNED BY JANE MCGOWN FLYNN. HOOKED BY NANCY BLOOD, OWEGO, NEW YORK, 2000.

WHEN YOU HOOK PANSIES, IT is important to remember what author and garden lover E. A. Bowles called their "wonderfully friendly and cheerful… face[s]." A pansy even has a nose— a small triangle in the flower's center. I put a single row of green on the two upper edges of this nose and a single row of another hue on the bottom, then fill the triangle with a warm, soft white.

Pansies are often drawn with a dominant, forward-facing bottom petal, which is hooked first. This petal has whiskers, lines of color extending from the center toward the outer edge. Do not fill this area with a solid mass of dark color. Instead, use rays of color spreading from the bottom of the nose toward the edge in graceful arcs both long and short. It is important to keep the rays pointed at the ends, so turn the ends of the strips at a right angle to the row of hooking to make a point.

Do not always use a dark value for the whiskers. You can also use a color found elsewhere in the rug, including the greens from leaves. Some hybrid pansies no longer have prominent whiskers, but do have streaks of a different color. To hook these, use grayed values of a contrasting color rather than a dark or bright one.

Often the whiskers are shown close to the edges of this overlapping petal. To achieve the necessary contrast, use the darkest values of the swatch (or strip) in just a few places in the petal's interior and in the spaces between the whiskers, rather than at the edges of the petal. Work through to the lighter values of the swatch; use the middle and light-middle values on the sides of the petal near the nose. By using the lightest color near the front edge of the petal, the middle values on the sides, and some dark in the center near the whiskers, you will achieve a certain amount of perspective as well as proper shading.

Use the same technique to hook the two side petals and their whiskers. If these whiskers are dark, they will lie nicely under the edges of the first petal. If they are medium in tone, you may need to do additional shadowing. Your eye will tell you what is needed.

Feel free to change colors on the two back petals since pansies are often multihued. Where these petals dip down into the V of the other petals they should be very dark; think both shadow and perspective. However, do not extend that first, darkest line all the way to the outside of the petal—use lighter darks (value 5, 6, or 7) to reach the outer edge. This will soften the shading and prevent a harsh, eye-grabbing line in the work.

NANCY BLOOD

PANSY ON SHAKER BOX, 10" DIAMETER, #3-CUT WOOL ON MONK'S CLOTH. DESIGNED BY JANE MCGOWN FLYNN. HOOKED BY NANCY BLOOD, OWEGO, NEW YORK, 2000.

THE FLOWERS

Poinsettia

AT LAST, 38" x 30", #3-CUT WOOL ON MONK'S CLOTH. DESIGNED AND HOOKED BY CONNIE CHARLESON, NEW PORT RICHEY, FLORIDA, 1998.

RED AND PINK POINSETTIAS bring welcome color to winter days. A poinsettia may appear to have large flowers, but in truth those are the leaves (called bracts); the flowers are the small yellow clusters surrounded by the bracts.

I used three reds in my *At Last*: a pink-red (see formula 1 below), a deep red (formula 2), and a bright red (formula 3), using all three in each poinsettia, with one being predominant in each. I used the open pan dyeing method, Cushing dyes, and 6 pieces of 6" x 12" white wool for dyeing 6 values, simmering the wool for at least 45 minutes.

First hook the flowers as circles of bright yellow with a dot of red in each center. Surround them with dark green. Then hook the small bracts surrounding the flower. It is not necessary to use all the values in these small bracts. Starting with value 4 or 5, hook a vein through the center, about halfway up, and then hook each consecutive shade from dark to light at the edge with value 1 at the tips. (My illustration uses colors rather than numbers to indicate the placement of values. Each color represents a *value* of a swatch—not the hue you are to use.)

FORMULA #1—PINK-RED

1 $1/2$ tsp Scarlet
$1/2$ tsp Cherry
$1/4$ tsp Garnet

FORMULA #2—DEEP RED

1 $1/2$ tsp Scarlet
1 tsp Turkey Red
$1/4$ tsp Mulberry

FORMULA #3—BRIGHT RED

1 $1/2$ tsp Turkey Red
$1/8$ tsp Maroon
$1/16$ tsp Yellow

POINSETTIA #1

PETAL #I

PETAL #II

GREEN

GREEN

PETAL #III

PETAL #IV

Lightest
2
3 Green
4
5
6 Darkest

CENTER VERY DARK GREEN
Flower ACTUAL COLOR ABOUT #15

POINSETTIA LEAF VEINS ± ABOUT shadow GREEN #1 ± 2 g swatch #3

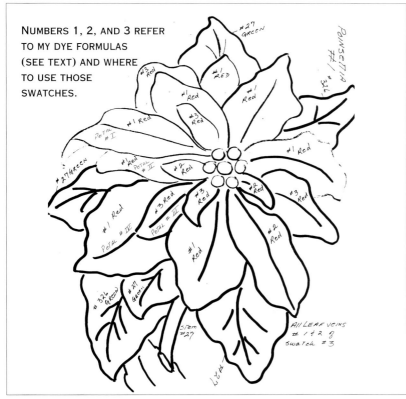

NUMBERS 1, 2, AND 3 REFER TO MY DYE FORMULAS (SEE TEXT) AND WHERE TO USE THOSE SWATCHES.

#27 GREEN

POINSETTIA #1 #32L

#3 Red

#1 Red

#1 Red

PETAL #I #1 Red

#27GREEN

#3 Red

#2 Red

#1 Red

PETAL #II

#1 Red

#3 Red

#2 Red

#1 Red

PETAL #IV

#3 Red

PETAL #III

#3 Red

#1 Red

#2 Red

#3 Red

#32L GREEN

#27 Green

Stem #27

All LEAF VEINS #1 ± 2 g swatch #3

Next hook bract I, the top bract. Hook value 6 halfway up the center of it, with three or four loops on either side of this vein. Put value 5 above it to within 1/2" of the edge and finish with 4. Hooking one side of the bract at a time, put in the increasingly lighter values.

The size of the bract determines how many rows of each value to use in it. The small bracts use just one row of each value; the large, two or three. The more rows of values 4, 5, and 6, the darker the bract.

It's better to hook adjacent bracts rather than to skip around hooking all the top or bottom ones. Hooking them in order (I, II, III, IV, etc.) makes it easier to judge where to place shadows and what's needed to separate the bracts.

To separate bract I from II, hook at least two rows of value 6 between I and the small center bract to about 1" from the edge of II. Value 5 follows. This establishes a shadow. Use values 4, 3, and 2 after 5 and at least two rows of 1 at the tip.

Hook bract III next, hooking from dark to light. Bract IV is larger, so hook several rows of each value in it. If you make the bract edges slightly jagged they'll look more realistic.

CONNIE CHARLESON

Poppy

SWEET SIXTEEN, DETAIL. DESIGNED BY JANE MCGOWN FLYNN. HOOKED BY HELEN CONNELLY. SEE PAGE 16.

ONE OF THE MOST RUFFLED of flowers, the poppy presents particular challenges to the rug hooker because its delicate, papery petals are generally one color. As with most flowers, begin your hooking in the center. A real poppy's center appears black, but its true iridescence is best conveyed with deep purple wool rather than black. Hook the stamens in a medium blue and outline them with brown or purple.

Also hook the fringed edge of the petals in a medium to dark blue. You can hook the fringe a little higher than the rest of the petal to convey texture, but don't make it a tight geometric shape. Instead, make it a softly serrated circle and use fingering to place deep purple here and there. This surrounding line of purple should be irregularly shaped; you can also use it to intensify the shadow at the base of the outside petals. Any

time a dark line is used to depict deepest shadow it should not be continuous, but instead broken

"BUT PLEASURES ARE LIKE POPPIES SPREAD—
YOU SEIZE THE FLOW'R, ITS BLOOM IS SHED...."

ROBERT BURNS

into segments of three to six loops and blended with other dark colors in the shaded area.

Next, hook the turned-over edges of the petals (known as turnovers) in the lighter values of your swatch. Although a transitional swatch is recommended for hooking poppies (it goes from the light of one color to the dark of another), dip-dyed wool that progresses quickly from light to dark can also be used. Hook the uneven edge of the petal, then shade back to the base of the turnover with three to four values. On the inside of the petal, right under the turnover, hook one row of another color—in a medium to dark value—from one of the other flowers in the rug. Doing this carries colors around the piece and makes the entire rug more interesting.

Hooking the forwardmost petal first, shade the area from the dark purple center to the area under the turnover with your darker values, going a little lighter toward the sides of the petal. Next, shade the petal underneath in those places where the topmost petal would cast a shadow. To create ruffles, highlight those folds in the petal that protrude and shade

the valleys with darker values. The farther back the petals are from the viewer, the darker the shading at the base to continue the impression that they are behind the lighter petals in the front.

Although hooking one row of background around a motif is always recommended, you give your poppy more impact by leaving just the tiniest amount of space between it and the background.

HELEN CONNELLY
(WITH SANDRA BROWN)

WHAT'S YOUR DESIRE?

There are many stylistic ways to hook a flower: dramatically or subtly, stylistically or realistically, with few or many details, or in a painterly or graphic fashion. What's your desire or intent? The feeling you wish to achieve will help you develop your approach. Whatever the inspiration, keep your interpretation constant throughout the piece. This will give your piece the consistency it needs to convey your intent to the viewer.

The feeling you wish to achieve will often dictate the colors you will use and their intensity. To achieve a realistic, dramatic effect, have a palette with strong contrasts. To show attention to detail, use a #3 or 4 cut of wool. To achieve a painterly approach, don't rely completely upon swatches or evenly dyed wool. Use color flows, spots, and odds and ends of related colors.—*Susan Higgins*

THE FLOWERS

Rose

THRESHOLD BEAUTIES, 28" x 19", #3-CUT WOOL ON BURLAP. DESIGNED BY MARGARET HUNT MASTERS. HOOKED BY NANCY BLOOD, OWEGO, NEW YORK, 1998.

ROSES APPEAR MORE OFTEN ON patterns than any other flower; that's why they can make or break a rug. Each petal must be clearly defined, and that takes great care and the ability to think one petal ahead.

Always do the turned-over portions of petals (turnovers) first, in very light values. Use shading to fill them if they're large, or a single value if small. Make the turnovers more appealing by using in them a color from something else in the rug. The turnovers in the white and pink rose in *Floral Potpourri* use the lavender from the rug's tulip. In *Threshold Beauties*, the rose's turnovers were hooked with wool dyed with the same formula used in the orange lily.

Think of roses as cup-and-saucer flowers and start with the cup. Place an amoeba-shaped highlight off center in the topmost petal. Surround that highlight with succeeding values. Never go darker than value 5 of an 8-value swatch. This is especially impor-tant on the bottom of the cup, since the darkest values will appear in the saucer. With the sec-ond petal, I start with value 2; if there is a third petal in the cup, I start that with value 3. Regardless of the number of cup petals, I still go no deeper than value 5. If you're working on a very large rose, use 12 values and give your-self a little leeway.

It is always necessary to have a definite shadow area to define petals. However, be careful about extending a shadow line all the way from edge to edge, for doing so will make the area too dark and hard. Hook the darkest value to start, then add increasingly lighter values to soften the spot. Remember, you don't have to use the lightest value to highlight or the darkest to create a shadow. The exception to this rule comes with hooking white flowers; due to the soft chroma of their swatches and the need to sharply define their light petals, you may need to extend that darkest value to the edge of the underneath petal. A little judicious beveling, or using a skinnier strip, will soften this dark line.

As you move into the cup your values should darken and even gray. A rose has a heart that

FLORAL POTPOURRI, DETAIL. DESIGNED BY JANE MCGOWN FLYNN. HOOKED BY NANCY BLOOD. SEE THE ENTIRE RUG ON PAGE 44.

needs dark values. You can often introduce something from another flower or even a leaf into this dark heart, if it's called for.

Sometimes it's difficult to distinguish the back petals of the cup from the back petals of the saucer. In my white rose the cup looks like a cup. My red rose has just three rather amorphous petals behind the two large petals; I treated them as the back part of the cup. Both roses' back cup petals were mock shaded—one value following another in sequence—giving them a pronounced, streaky effect.

The saucer of the rose acts as a support for the cup; therefore, it has to be visually strong enough to do just that. I put my darkest values under the cup, but not all the way around it. When I was first taught to hook a rose, I was told to use all the values in the swatch on both sections of the

> ## "Live now, believe me, wait not till tomorrow;
> ## Gather the roses of life today."
>
> Pierre de Ronsard

blossom, then divide the cup and saucer with a line of very dark color between the two. That line looked like a grin to me, so I don't do that anymore, nor do I put in one line of dark and one of light and then fill in the rest of a petal with the middle values. That's not wrong, but it isn't interesting. Everything we do is predicated on contrast—light and dark, highlight and shadow—and a great blob of medium tones filling something is hardly that.

In both roses, the front petals of the saucer are mock shaded. I treat the back petals differently, depending on their size. If the petals are shallow, as they are in the red rose, I use layering—I place the values in rows, defining each area as I go and completing one at a time. Never judge an unfinished motif. Complete the whole element, then go back and make corrections.

The white rose's back petals are mock shaded since they are larger. Occasionally in a white rose I slip in a darker value, which allows me a little pleat or fold in the petal.

Through the years I have taught and hooked dozens of roses, but I don't think I've ever done any of them the same way. I try, and teach, new things all the time, and thank goodness my students generally have the patience to let me do so. Don't be afraid to try new techniques yourself on this beautiful, popular flower.

Nancy Blood

Age & Environment

Flowers have an age and are affected by their environment. A bud has a deep, intense color and is generally free from the ravages of age. A newly opened flower is fresh and clean, but still somewhat deep in tone, while a fully opened flower may be faded from the sun. An aging flower may be somewhat wilted and have brown spots on it from rot, rust, or insect damage.

These innuendoes provide you with clues as to how to hook your piece. If you are hooking a single flower, you may want it to be a perfect or unusual specimen. If you are hooking a group of flowers, it may be more interesting to vary their age and condition, so you can vary your palette and interpretation. This will make the piece more visually alluring.—*Susan Higgins*

THE FLOWERS

Sunflower

SUNFLOWER PANEL, 12" X 29", #3-CUT WOOL ON BURLAP.
DESIGNED BY CAROL KASSERA. HOOKED BY MARLETA
ANDERSON, NEWARK VALLEY, NEW YORK, 1998.

SUNFLOWERS ARE CHEERFUL flowers that now come in many colors and varieties. I, however, chose to put the old-fashioned yellow variety in my interpretation of *Sunflower Panel*.

I used two yellow-gold formulas for the flowers. Each swatch had 8 values, with value 1 being the lightest. For the first and third flowers I used one swatch, and for the second and fourth the other. The second and fourth flowers also have some of the darker swatch in them to unify all four flowers. The leaves were hooked with blue-green swatches left over from other rugs. The background was dyed with a plum formula from my teacher, Nancy Blood.

Hook the center of a sunflower first. Make a smile shape just inside the edge of the center and a bit to one side, curving it two-thirds of the way around the center. I used leftovers, including greens, browns, rusts, purple, blue, and a touch of a white tweed. Follow the smile to fill the entire center. Stay inside the lines or the center will grow too big.

The fun part of hooking these flowers is shading each petal differently. A sunflower is open and flat, so its center casts very little shadow on the petals. The petals are not very close together, so there are few shadows on the edges. Look for the petals that are on top or in front of the rest of the flower and hook them first, using the lighter values. Make folds and ripples by placing darker values toward the center. For instance, hook with value 3 a third of the way up the center of a petal, and fill around it with value 2, then 1 to the edge. On another petal, where there might be a shadow from the neighboring petal, start with value 8 against the light edge of the petal above it and work out to the edge using successively lighter values as there is room.

When a petal has a turnover at its tip, hook the turnover with some of the darker values from another swatch. Make the dark edge of the turnover extend some distance down the edge of the rest of the petal so the turnover does not look as if it is an extra piece stuck onto the end.

Flat, open flowers are difficult to hook because they need to be given definition through shading and the use of color, rather than by following a shape with highlights and shadows as you would in other flowers, such as roses. Try different ways to make each petal distinct and make the flower come alive. The sunflower is a good blossom on which to test your creativity.

MARLETA ANDERSON

THE FLOWERS

Throated Flowers

Buckingham, 72" x 44", #3- and 4-cut wool on 2 x 2 cotton. Designed by Jane McGown Flynn. Hooked by Helen Connelly, Northport, New York. unfinished.

UNDERSTANDING THE construction of throated flowers is critical to hooking them realistically. As the name implies, throated flowers have a trumpet shape: narrow where the flower meets the stem and widening to a flared blossom that turns outward and under at the edge. The underturned petal casts a shadow on the upper neck.

Many throated flowers are hooked in several values of one color, light to dark. The two portions of the flower, the neck and face, are hooked separately.

Hook the neck first, making it darker or lighter than the face, depending on the light source. Generally, if light hits the face, it casts a shadow on the neck. To separate the two portions of the flower, use sharply contrasting values of color where the neck meets the face.

Shade the neck carefully to make it look rounded, by putting in dark values at the edges and light down the center for a highlight. The shading between the highlight and edges must be smooth and subtle. With the

lightest value of your swatch, hook the highlight lengthwise from the face to the base of the flower. Stop the highlight just short of either end of the neck, and put in a few loops of a darker value to create a shadow.

Using a darker value, hook both edges of the neck vertically. Fill in the rest of the neck with middle values, hooking them lengthwise to elongate it. Use as many as you can fit comfortably in the neck. The shading should be so subtle that you can't count the number of values easily.

For the face, choose your values carefully, particularly for the edge so it is distinct from the neck, the background, and other elements that touch the flower. Depending on the light source, you may choose to shade the face light to dark from the center outward or from the edge inward.

As with the neck, hook the extreme values first, then fill in the middle values. Hook the face from the center outward to make the flower open up. Place some darker loops to mimic folds.

When it is turned toward you, the far inside of a face is more visible than the near inside. Therefore, the shading should extend farther down into the flower on the far side. On the near side, show the inner edge of the face by hooking a row of darker values. Then, shade from that edge outward to where the petal turns over the neck.

The best way to learn how to hook any flower is to study a real-life example. Take advantage of spring and study newly opened blossoms. Turn the flower so the light hits it from different angles, and note how the shading changes. Better yet, make shaded drawings and build your own reference library of flowers.

JEANNE FALLIER

THE FLOWERS

Tulip

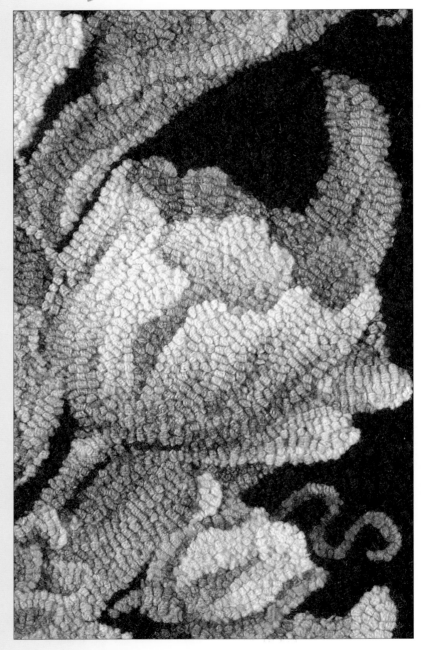

yellow, blue, or soft green. Dipping the wool into two or three dye baths creates a sequence of layered colors that emerges as the tulip petal is hooked from top to bottom. In casserole dyeing, a piece of wool approximately five times the length of the petal is gently painted with different colors of dye, either in bands from top to bottom or in segments, such as the four corners. The trick to casserole dyeing is to end up with a piece of wool that includes a range from light to dark values. The blending of colors that will naturally occur in the middle is desirable. This blending shows up beautifully in the final hooking of the tulip if you lay out the strips in sequence on a piece of tape (to keep them in place) and then hook them in that order.

With your lightest values hook the most prominent petal first. The first row of hooking must be down the center. This center line establishes the direction of the hooking (which should follow the curve of the petal). Hook it with a strip from

ALTHOUGH REAL TULIPS COME in a variety of colors, hooked tulips are even more colorful, for they can bear hints of hues from the other flowers in a rug. They present the perfect opportunity for using dip-dyed and casserole-dyed wools.

In dip dyeing, your wool can be any base color, such as pink, the assembled cut wool.

Next hook to the right and then the left of this first line, using the adjacent strands of wool from the right and left of your taped arrangement. Occasionally shorten strips slightly at the beginning of a row to control color or to convey the stripes many tulips have. On the short sides of a petal you may need to pull up extra long loops and cut them off to quickly get to a color farther down a strip.

Hook the stamens and anthers next (ideally each a different color). Here is an excellent opportunity to place colors from elsewhere in the rug. Otherwise, provide enough contrast for them to be seen against the background of the tulip. For example, hook the stamens in a dark purple (not black) and the anthers a dark rust if the center is light or medium; or stamens a light green and anthers a rust if the center is dark.

HELEN CONNELLY
(WITH SANDRA BROWN)

SWEET SIXTEEN.
DESIGNED BY JANE McGOWN FLYNN. HOOKED BY HELEN CONNELLY. SEE PAGE 16.

Water Lily

PHOTOGRAPH BY JEANNE FALLIER

WATER LILY, 14" DIAMETER, #3-CUT WOOL ON BURLAP. DESIGNED AND HOOKED BY JEANNE FALLIER, WESTFORD, MASSACHUSETTS, 1981.

SOME YEARS AGO I DREW A water lily design for a guild project. In hooking my own interpretation of it I decided I wanted to do a water lily with petals shading from pale to deep pink, using a swatch dyed with Cushing's American Beauty dye. There's a touch of blue in the deeper values but not enough to become purple in tone.

I used the same swatches in the buds, but put more of the

deeper values in them. The smaller the bud, the deeper its color. The shadow lines in the buds show the addition of that bit of blue to the dye. I followed the contours of the petals as I hooked.

Leftover pieces of pale green and gold became the stamens in the center, topped with dots of the deepest pink-purple of the swatch. The leaves are a mix of greens I had on hand (washed together, with some beige wool added to the batch), such as blue-green for the darkest parts and an olive hue, almost a green-beige, for light areas. Light portions of the leaves were outlined in a dark value to set them off from the aqua-teal background.

In order to have contrast between the design and the background, I hooked the entire background horizontally. I also mixed values of aqua and teal in it to resemble the color of water, hooked into place in a hit-and-miss fashion, but with deeper tones behind the flowers and leaves to suggest shadows.

The same procedure can be followed for a white water lily or lotus. Use pale values of green for the shadows and small amounts of pure white for the highlights.

I incorporated my initials into the design and added the guild's name as well. My water lily project became a chair pillow, with medium-teal velvet for both the backing and the edges of the velvet-covered cording.

JEANNE FALLIER

White Flowers

FLORAL POTPOURRI, 19" x 27", #3-CUT WOOL ON 2 X 2 COTTON. DESIGNED BY JANE MCGOWN FLYNN. HOOKED BY NANCY BLOOD, OWEGO, NEW YORK, 1998.

JUST AS WHITE LIGHT BROKEN by a prism reveals a multitude of colors in the rainbow, white flowers can bear other hues, too. Hooking a white flower is really no different than hooking any other color if you take the time to make sure your choice of wool will get your artistic message across.

The white flowers in my interpretation of *Floral Potpourri* used just six Cushing dyes, which were dyed repeatedly in varying amounts over different colors of wool. The baby's breath and rose were hooked with white wool dyed to 8 values with Cushing's Plum and Woodrose. The tulip and violets bear those two dyes plus Navy, and the gardenia and campanulas were done with Silver Gray Green, Old Ivory, and Khaki Drab.

To have the viewer's eye travel around the piece, I tucked the tulip color into the rose and had the gardenia and tulip trade colors. I changed this a bit with the smaller flowers, tying the baby's breath and gardenia together, and the violets and campanulas with the rose. I could have put all the colors in every flower by matching hue intensities and not values.

Swatches are wonderful for hooking delicate, elegant designs. When I dye swatches, they become mottled, and this helps develop the nuances found in finely detailed patterns. Each value has its own place in the strategies involved in shading. By placing highlights at different angles and heights in a petal, you can tip, turn, and bend that petal in an infinite number of ways. The values allow you to separate the petals from each other yet still unite them in the whole blossom.

Notice that the campanula and rose have turned-over edges on some of their petals. Extend a line of color along the edges of the turnover and into the rest of the petal; just filling in the turnover will make it look like the petal is wearing a hat. I usually try to exaggerate the extended line, letting it simply die away into the motif. I turn the last loop of the strand of wool so that it's at right angles to the rest of the loops, making a point.

The baby's breath flowers were outlined, then filled with increasingly darker values until I reached the center. Little posies like these are fun to do because you can introduce hues in them to balance your color plan.

Support white flowers with rich backgrounds and significant leaves. By putting a dark background behind light flowers, no edges will be lost over time and the blossoms will remain preeminent.

NANCY BLOOD

ADDITIONAL INSTRUCTION AND DESIGN HINTS

Primitive Flowers

1790 Table Mat, 22" x 18 3/4", #6-cut wool on linen. Designed by Marion Ham. Hooked by Betty McClentic, Warwick, Rhode Island, 1997.

PRIMITIVE FLOWERS BY THEIR very nature present different problems than those hooked realistically. Think of them in terms of art: Realistically hooked flowers can be compared to fine art; those hooked in a primitive manner might be compared to modern art. The former speaks plainly about what it represents, whereas the latter relies more on an impression. Primitive art often is form in its simplest terms.

Today we are blessed with an abundance of materials, both new and recycled, with which we can make rugs. The question becomes how to best use these materials to create the rug you desire. Do you want a rug that has a muted, antique look or a brighter, contemporary appearance? Primitive rugs, more than those that use fine cuts of wool and careful shading, create a mood. For instance, a rug with a dark background and medium-value details gives a moody, somber impression, while one made with bright, warm colors creates a happy look. The use of wide cuts of wool seems to underscore the mood created by the color.

Your cut of wool need not be wide for your rug to be primitive, although that is the generally accepted belief. Many rug hookers prefer wide-cut strips because they find their rugs work up faster with them (although pulling wide strips through backing can be hard on your hands and shoulders). Some use hand-cut strips, as the unevenness adds to the handmade look.

Once you determine what cut you prefer, consider how you will hook the flowers in your rug. Should you outline them? Here are some guidelines. If there needs to be more definition between a flower's color and the background's, either because the values are too similar or dissimilar, outlining can separate them or create a bridge between the two. Sometimes the color you have chosen for a flower is a little dull or too bright; the right outline color could enhance it or calm it. For example, a yellow flower becomes more vibrant if it's outlined with purple, its complement. The same yellow flower edged with khaki will look softer.

Outlining a flower's many petals will keep them separated.

WINCHESTER, 44" x 88", #6-CUT WOOL ON RUG WARP. DESIGNED BY JANE MCGOWN FLYNN. HOOKED BY BETTY MCCLENTIC, WARWICK, RHODE ISLAND, 1996.

Use a double outline on the flowers that are the most important ones in your piece. To unify motifs, outline your flowers with colors from other details in your rug.

There are other ways to keep a multipetaled flower from becoming a blob. Hook the odd petals in bright or dark values and the even ones in dull or light. The small flowers in *Antique Runner* are examples of this technique. Perhaps in your rug it would be more interesting to make the odd petals a different color altogether from the even ones. In my *1790 Table Mat*, a different, deeper color in the lower area separates the two

floral shapes. There is no outlining of any of the flowers in this piece.

Spot dyeing or overdyeing are two easy ways to adjust or change the color of your materials. The uneven spread of color in spot dyeing can create texture in your hooked work. Overdyeing natural, peach, yellow, blue, beige, and pink with Cushing's Mahogany dye was a way to create unity in *Winchester*. Except for the blue flowers, all the floral details in this rug were done with pieces of these overdyed pastels. They had been crowded into the same large pot with the dye, stirred a little, then allowed to absorb the dye. This

gave me a wonderful assortment of related colors to play with.

Swatches can be used in primitive rugs if you separate the values. I feel that swatches used in sequence for shading, no matter the size of the cut, are not appropriate for primitive work.

You can also create a primitive floral without dyeing. Mixing slightly different pieces of a color gives a nice variation that looks dyed when hooked in. The large flowers on the *Antique Runner* are an assortment of similar undyed pieces hooked randomly. As-is plaids and other textured wool add interest to a hooked flower, whether

placed in the center, or petals, or as an outline.

Since the strips you will be hooking with will probably be wide, the direction of your hooked lines becomes important. I like to hook my rows in the direction in which the flower grows—from the center outward, in the case of a throated flower, or in the shape of the petals, in the case of a rounded blossom. By matching your hooking direction to the growth of the flower, the character and form of the flower is realized without shading.

If you have a problem trying to decide which way a flower is growing, forget that what you are working on is a flower and treat it as merely a shape. See it as round, or long and pointed, or one shape on top of another. This method can give you a new way of seeing and a different approach to your work.

For the most part, hooking primitive flowers is easy. Just keep in mind that the primitive style is the simplest way to illustrate a flower in hooked form. If you use interesting materials and hook in a direction that supports its shape you should be satisfied with your result.

BETTY McCLENTIC

Designing a Floral Rug

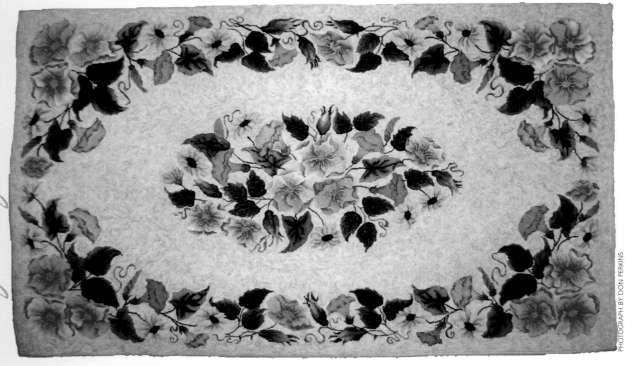

WAYSIDE MEMORIES, 50" x 30", #3-CUT WOOL ON BURLAP. DESIGNED BY PEARL K. McGOWN. HOOKED BY MARLETA ANDERSON, NEWARK VALLEY, NEW YORK, 1992.

PHOTOGRAPH BY DON PERKINS

THE PROCESS OF DESIGNING A floral hooked rug pattern requires several considerations. You need to select the flowers you'll want and the design format, and from there pay attention to balance, continuity, and flow. As a commercial rug designer, I must be concerned with pleasing the public, but you need only please yourself. Nonetheless, the steps I take to design a floral are the same you should take, too.

Suppose you want to develop a design to hook for your adult child. You want to include in this special project the birth flowers for all four of her children (your grandchildren). The design will incorporate roses, water lilies, violets, and sweet peas, the flowers of their birth months. Your first task is to collect as many visual aids as possible. Get pictures of all the flowers from several different angles and in different proportions to other flowers. Seed catalogs, calendars, wallpaper, and textile samples are excellent sources.

Next, select the design format:

1. A bouquet center with a scroll border.

2. A wreath of flowers in the center with each of the flowers in a different corner.

3. A garland floral border motif with a plain center.

You can also use whatever other format you feel will satisfy your design. Your choice depends upon where the rug will be used. Number 1 can be used in the center of a room, at a doorway, or at the hearth in a more formal room. Number 2 can be used as above, but also in a bedroom before a bureau or by the bed. Number 3

HARMONY, 70" X 35", #3-CUT WOOL ON MONK'S CLOTH. DESIGNED BY JANE MCGOWN FLYNN. HOOKED BY SUZANNE PETTY, KINGSWOOD, TEXAS, 1994.

works well beneath a coffee table.

Consider the width of the strips of wool that you plan on using for the rug. I prefer a #3 cut for fine floral rugs. Make each flower of an appropriate size to accommodate six to eight values in each petal for dramatic shading. If I were designing the above-mentioned commemorative floral, I would make the roses and water lilies at least 7" in diameter, the sweet peas no more than 3" in diameter, and the violets just under 2". All of the foliage would be a size compatible with the flowers.

Balance provides opportunity for colors to be carried throughout the design. You want to be able to repeat colors from a center bouquet to the surrounding border, whether it is a geometric (like a fence or fret) or a scroll. Balance the center bouquet by repeating the flowers and buds triangularly or diagonally opposite one another. If you were to place

all of the roses on one end and all of the water lilies on the other end, one end will appear heavier when color is applied and the design will be unbalanced.

Usually a bouquet will have one leading lady with supporting flowers accompanying her. The actual design may have two different flowers of the same strength (the rose and water lily), but when it's hooked only one should dominate. In our commemorative rug the leading lady will depend upon the background color. On a dark background the light water lily will dominate and the more colorful rose will play a supporting role.

I start drawing a design by placing a T-square in the center of my paper and measuring to the edges of the pattern (let's say this commemorative one will be 33" x 55"). Then I sketch an oval that will be filled with the bouquet. I

leave an appropriate amount of plain border (about 2" for this size pattern), and sketch the scroll, geometric frame, or corner motifs.

Continuity in the design is the next consideration. To be consistent in a rug with spring flowers, put in secondary flowers that are in bloom at the same time; for example, irises and tulips accompanied by crocuses and pussy willows, or roses and lilies with daisies and morning glories. This does not apply to the commemorative design we are discussing, however, for you might have had a December child's flower (holly) to incorporate with summer's water lilies.

Floral rugs should have a good flow. Each type of flower should be accompanied by the appropriate foliage. Flow is related to continuity in that the blossoms should be placed in a natural pattern. Avoid harsh or long lines. Interrupt long

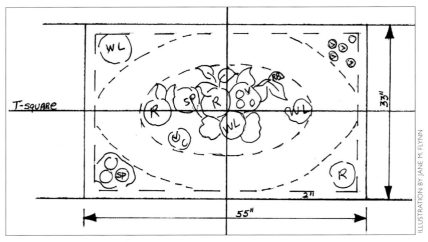

ILLUSTRATION BY JANE M. FLYNN

ADA PATTERN. DESIGNED BY PEARL K. MCGOWN.

Seven Sisters has seven different flowers in the center bouquet, a different flower for each of the girls in her family—rose, dahlia, lily, tulip, dogwood, pansy, and morning glory—surrounded by a strong leafy scroll. However, the opportunity to balance this design comes in the color planning.

Confer with fellow hookers to get their opinion of your design before you begin to hook. Probably the most frequent error I have observed in designing is that of proportion. I once saw a lady hooking a pattern of her beloved cat, the hooked cat being only slightly larger than the real cat. When the rug was finished the cat was well hooked, but the small creature looked lost in the middle of a large, unimaginative, hit-and-miss background.

Don't worry about realism in your flower drawings. You are attempting to make a beautiful accessory for your home. One lady once accused Pearl of doing a hatchet job on a flower. The lady was a botanist, and she pointed out that the hooked flower was missing a petal the real flower has. Remember that you are an artist creating these flowers for your own enjoyment, and designing a floral rug can be quite rewarding.

JANE MCGOWN FLYNN

stems and strap leaves with a bud or overlapping leaf.

Once your commemorative's center bouquet is filled with all the flowers, drawn at a couple of different angles to make them interesting, plan the corners. In each corner place just one of the flowers and its foliage. I would put the rose and the water lily in diagonally opposing corners because of their similar size; so too with the violets and sweet peas. Consider the location of the flowers in the center bouquet when you set the corner flowers. You do not want to have a rose at the edge of the center

bouquet next to a rose in the corner.

I can remember as a child watching my grandmother designing. When she thought she was all done, she would place a penny on each flower of the same variety. She would repeat the procedure for all varieties in the design, making sure that there was enough distance between each repeat so the pattern didn't get too heavy in any one area with a particular flower. If there was a clustering of any one flower, she would alter the pattern.

Not every floral rug is balanced. For instance, my grandmother's

Dyeing for Flowers

MANY PEOPLE ENJOY DYEING their own wool for floral rugs. Here are some formulas suitable for flowers that were developed by color expert Maryanne Lincoln. (Some of these formulas are from her book *Recipes From the Dye Kitchen, Edition II* in the Framework Series published by *Rug Hooking* magazine.)

JAR DYENG

EQUIPMENT & MATERIALS

- Enamel, stainless steel, or glass roaster, canner, or refrigerator pan large enough to hold six to eight 1-quart jars
- 6 to 8 wide-mouth quart jars
- 1-cup glass measuring cup
- Dye spoons
- Cushing acid dyes or PRO Chem wash-fast acid dyes
- Tongs
- Lined rubber gloves
- Uniodized salt
- White vinegar (5 percent)
- Long-handled spoon
- Small enamel pan to dissolve dyes
- Synthrapol (a liquid detergent for wetting wool, available from PRO Chem)
- Six to eight 3" x 12" pieces of wool[1]
- Hot tap water

DIRECTIONS

1 Soak the wool in hot water with a drop of Synthrapol. If you have hard water, use a bit more Synthrapol. Set the soaking wool aside.

2 Measure the dry ingredients of your formula into the small enamel pan. Add a small amount of cold water to make a paste. Add $3/4$ cup of hot tap water and bring the mixture to a quick boil. Stir the mixture and pour it into the 1-cup measure. Add hot water to make 1 cup of solution.

3 Arrange the jars in a roaster. Add hot tap water around the jars until they begin to float.

4 Stir the dye solution and pour $1/2$ cup of it into the first jar.

5 Refill the cup with hot tap water to the 1-cup level. Stir and pour $1/2$ cup into the next jar. Repeat this process (pouring off half the solution and adding more hot water to the 1-cup level) until all the jars contain solution. You will end up with $1/2$ cup of lightly tinted solution after pouring the last value. Don't pour it into the jar with the lightest solution. Save it for spot dyeing. It is not needed for this procedure.

6 Add $1/2$ teaspoon of salt to each jar. Then add extra water to each jar until each is about $2/3$ full. Put a drop of Synthrapol in each jar.

7 Gently squeeze some of the water out of the wet wool. (It is not necessary to rinse it unless you have used a wetting agent other than Synthrapol.) Use tongs to stir the wool into the jars of dye solution. Squish the wool up and down to force the dye solution through the wool. Move the tongs as you work to avoid leaving spots where the tongs grip the wool. Stir often while the swatch is processing.

8 Cover the roaster, not the individual jars. If you don't have a cover, loosely cover the pan with heavy foil.

9 Put the roaster over low heat. After about 10 minutes, remove the cover and stir the solution in each jar. Turn the heat down to a simmer. Stir the wool every 15 to 20 minutes. You can't stir too much. Make sure each piece of wool is completely submerged before you put the cover back over the jars.

10 Simmer the wool for one hour.[2] Then rinse the wool, starting with the lightest value. When the water rinses clear, hang the wool to dry. If the water does not rinse clear, put the wool in a small pan with 2 to 4 cups of water and 1 or 2 tablespoons of white vinegar. Bring it to a quick boil. Simmer the wool for a few minutes or until the water that drips from the wool is clear. If the wool is not one value darker compared to the previous strip, add some of the dye from its jar to the vinegar bath. Be careful, though. It is easy to get it too dark. If you use the vinegar bath for one value, you must do it for every value after that.

11 Dye solution left in jars can be used to spot dye odds and ends of scrap wool. Don't expect to get another swatch exactly like the one you just dyed.

12 Clean the jars thoroughly after use to avoid contaminating your next dye project. And remember, never use dye pots or utensils to cook food.

—Maryanne Lincoln

[1]**TO DYE MORE THAN ONE SWATCH** at a time, increase the number of pieces of wool, the strength of the dye solution, the amount of salt, and the amount of extra water you add to each jar. For example, to dye five swatches, add five times as much wool, dye solution, and salt. Add just enough water to make the wool easy to stir and to keep it submerged. The amount of extra water is not as important as the amount of materials, the strength of the dye solution, and the amount of salt. I add as much water as I can without overflowing the jars. Make sure to add about the same amount to each jar.

[2]**WHEN USING ACID DYES,** remove the wool after 30 to 40 minutes and stir 1 tablespoon of white vinegar into each jar. Then put the wool back into the jars. Simmer it for 30 minutes longer, stirring often. Remove the roaster from the heat, let the wool stand in the jars until it cools, and then finish as above.

FORMULAS

FOR EACH OF THE FORMULAS, follow the directions above to
dye a piece of 3" x 24" white or natural wool in each jar.

CUSHING FORMULAS

Blue-Purple Pansy
3/16 tsp Cherry
3/16 tsp Peacock
1/64 tsp Canary

Buttercup
3/4 tsp Canary
1/128 tsp Cherry
1/128 tsp Peacock

Foliage
1/2 tsp Canary
3/16 tsp Peacock
1/32 tsp Black
1/32 tsp Cherry

Lady Slipper
1/8 tsp Canary
1/128 tsp Peacock
1/128 tsp Black
3/8 tsp Cherry

Morning Glories #7a
1/8 tsp Peacock
1/64 tsp Cherry
1/128 tsp Canary

Mum Leaf Green #3a
3/32 tsp Peacock
5/16 tsp Canary
1/32 tsp Cherry
1/128 tsp Black

Rusty Tulip #5a
3/8 tsp Canary
1/16 tsp Cherry
1/128 tsp Peacock

PRO CHEM FORMULAS

Antique Rose
3/32 tsp #672 black
3/32 tsp #233 orange
3/32 tsp #338 red

Dusky Lilac
3/32 tsp #672 black
1/32 tsp #490 blue
1/32 tsp #338 red

Pansies #10a
3/16 tsp #338 red
3/16 tsp #490 blue
1/64 tsp #119 yellow

Red-Purple Pansy
3/8 tsp #338 red
1/8 tsp #490 blue
1/64 tsp #119 yellow
1/128 tsp #672 black

Sunflowers #12a
1/2 tsp #119 yellow
1/128 tsp #490 blue
1/64 tsp #338 red

Tropical Foliage
1/4 tsp #119 yellow
1/32 tsp #490 blue
3/128 tsp #338 red
1/128 tsp #672 black

Wisteria
3/32 tsp #672 black
1/64 tsp #490 blue
3/64 tsp #338 red

SPECIAL FORMULAS

It's easy to shade a flower with a swatch that goes from
a smoky dark version of a color to a very bright one.
The dark values create shadows and the light values
bring up the highlights. The formulas below build
from a weak gradation of black and require you to per-
form two steps.

Charcoal Rose (PRO Chem)
Step 1: 1/16 tsp #672 black
Dissolve the dye in 1 cup of boiling water and distribute the solution into 6 jars according to the jar dyeing
method.

Step 2: 1/32 tsp #338 red
            1/64 tsp #119 yellow
Dissolve the dyes in 1 cup of boiling water and add 2
1/2 tablespoons of the resulting solution to each jar.
Stir the solution in each jar and continue with jar dyeing to dye over 4 1/2" x 24" of white wool in each jar.

Charcoal Rose (Cushing)
Step 1: 1/32 tsp Black
Dissolve the dye in 1 cup of
boiling water and distribute the solution into 6 jars
according to the jar dyeing method.

Step 2: 1/32 tsp Cherry
            1/64 tsp Canary
Dissolve the dyes in 1 cup of boiling water and add 2
1/2 tablespoons of the solution to each jar. Stir the
solution in each jar and continue with jar dyeing to
dye over 4 1/2" x 24" of white wool in each jar.

Before you begin hooking a pattern, machine stitch two rows around the perimeter as a defense against fraying. Stitch the first row $1/4$" beyond what will be the hooked portion, and the second row $1/4$" beyond the first row. Overstitch each row of straight stitches with a row of zigzag stitches.

These basic instructions apply to hooking with all widths of woolen strips. Step 3, however, applies to hooking with narrow strips in #3, 4, and 5 cuts. (The number refers to the numerical designation of a cutter wheel on a fabric cutting machine. A #3 wheel cuts a strip $3/32$" wide; a #5 cuts a strip $5/32$" wide; a #8, $8/32$" or $1/4$" wide, and so on.) Refer to the section on hooking with wide strips for special tips on holding a hook when making a wide-cut rug.

1 Stretch the backing in a hoop or frame with the design side up. Sitting comfortably, rest the hoop or frame on a table or your lap. The thumbscrew of a hoop should be opposite you.

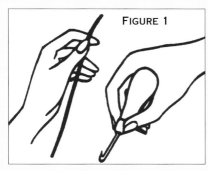

FIGURE 1

2 With your left hand (right hand if you're a leftie) hold the end of a woolen strand between your thumb and forefinger **(Figure 1)**.

3 With your right hand, hold the hook as if it were a pencil, with your fingertips on the metal collar as shown.

4 Hold the wool in your left hand and put it beneath the backing. With your right hand, push the hook down through the mesh. The shaft of the hook should touch your left forefinger and slide behind the woolen strip. Push the wool onto the barb with your left thumb.

5 Pull the end of the strip through to the front of the backing with the hook, to a height of about $1/2$".

6 Push the hook down through the backing a little to the left of the strip's end and catch the strip underneath. Pull up a $1/8$" loop, or as high as the strip is wide. To prevent pulling out the previous loop, lean the hook back toward the previous loop as you pull up another loop.

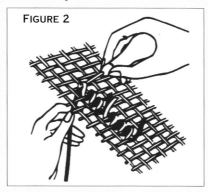

FIGURE 2

7 Working from right to left, make even loops that gently touch each other as in **Figure 2**. With fine strips, hook in almost every hole. Never put more than one loop in a hole.

8 When you reach the end of the woolen strip, pull the end up through the backing. Pull all ends through to the front as you hook. Tails on the back are untidy and can be easily pulled out.

9 Start the next strip in the same hole in which the last strip ended, again leaving a $1/2$" tail.

10 Trim the ends even with the loops after making several loops with the new strip.

11 Continue the hooking process until the pattern is complete. To keep the back of the rug from becoming lumpy, do not cross a row of hooking with another strip. Cut the strip and start again.

12 Practice the following exercises to achieve the proper rhythm and technique: (a) try hooking straight lines and wavy lines; (b) pack rows

FIGURE 3

against one another to form a pile as in **Figure 3**.

Even the most skilled rug hooker must pull out loops now and then. Individual strands can be removed easily, but loops in packed areas are harder to remove. Use the hook or a pair of tweezers. Strands may be re-used if they are not badly frayed, and the blank area of the backing may be hooked again.

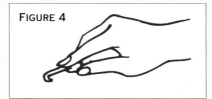

FIGURE 4

HOOKING WITH WIDE STRIPS

When hooking with wide strips ($1/4$" to $1/2$"), note that they pull up more easily if you hold the hook in the palm of your hand **(Figure 4)** and insert it into the backing at a sharper angle. (Some even prefer to hold the hook in this manner when working with narrow strips.) As with narrow strips, the shaft of the hook should rub the forefinger of your left hand and pass behind the woolen strip. The barb should hit your thumb, which pushes the wool onto the hook. Never loop the wool over the hook with your left hand; this will result in a lumpy back. If you cannot pick up the strip with your hook, the barb is not properly positioned.

HAPPY & STEVE DiFRANZA

Glossary

ANTHER—The part of a stamen that produces and contains pollen, found at the end of a stalk.

BRACTS—Leaves that lie underneath a flower or flower cluster.

CASSEROLE DYEING—A dyeing method in which wool is pleated or scrunched in a pan and several dye solutions are spooned over it in rows perpendicular to the selvage.

CHROMA—See Intensity.

CROSS-SWATCHING (ALSO KNOWN AS MULTISWATCHING)—Combining values from two or more closely related swatches.

CUSHING DYES—Acid dyes from W. Cushing & Company.

DIP DYEING—A dyeing method in which wool is dipped into dye solutions to produce a gradation from light to dark.

FINGERING—Laying in values in strokes of varying lengths, like the meshed fingers of two hands.

FLORETS—The small flowers that form a cluster or composite flower.

HUE—Color.

INTENSITY—The strength or saturation of a color; a color's brightness or dullness.

JAR DYEING—Dyeing a range of values in jars set in a pan of water.

MOCK SHADING—Laying in values of wool in sequential rows.

MULTISWATCHING—See Cross-swatching.

PADULA—A hooked flower that does not exist in nature.

PISTIL—The reproductive portion of a flower, consisting of an ovary, stigma, and style.

POISON—A bright or bold hue introduced into a pattern to add spark.

SEPALS—Modified leaves that form a cup at the base of a flower.

STAMEN—The pollen-producing organ of a flower, consisting of an anther and a filiment (stalk).

STROKING—See Fingering.

SWATCH—A set of dyed wool pieces that progress in value.

TRANSITION DYEING—Dyeing that produces a transition from one color to another.

TRANSITIONAL SWATCH—A swatch that progresses from the light value of one color to the dark value of another.

TURNOVER—The turned-over portion of a petal or leaf.

VALUE—The lightness or darkness of a color.